I0102279

Your Vote Matters:
"The Easy Way to use Your Power"

J.W. Cherry III

Foreword by: Glen E. Smith Jr.

Copyright © 2014
Your Vote Matters:
"The Easy Way to use Your Power"
J.W. Cherry III

Printed in the United States of America
ISBN 978-0-9904624-6-0

DEDICATION

To all those that have dedicated their energy to the civil rights movement of yesterday and today.

ACKNOWLEDGEMENTS

Thank you God for giving me the will and the way. I thank my loving wife, Patsy for believing in me. I thank my children; Candice, April and John IV, for pushing me. I thank my granddaughter, Alissa and the loving memory of my grandson, William - you are both my greatest legacies. To my parents, John Jr. and Octavia, thank you for inspiring me to make the world a better place.

FOREWORD

Remember the past – lead the future: How can we do our part? As we partake of the benefits that our civil rights martyrs fought for; let us value the power that we possess to keep the civil rights movement thriving, with the focus of unity, justice, inclusion and eminence. Your basic civic duty is to vote. The only cost is your time.

In 2014, we are in a pivotal time in American history, as we celebrate the 50th Anniversary of the 1964 Civil Rights Act; It is the 50th Anniversary of the March on Washington for Jobs and Freedom, the 49th year of the 1965 Voting Rights Act and it has been 60 years since the landmark case of Brown v. Board of Education of Topeka, Kansas.

During the past 2 decades I have served in the military as a USMC Military Police Corporal and as a South Carolina Sheriff Deputy, I currently own a Private investigation Company "Elect Protection Group" in the state of Florida. I have witnessed the effects of the legal system on our youth from multiple levels. Once our young are placed in the system they are doomed.

Upon paying their debt to society they have lost the right to vote, an ability to obtain employment and they are given a bus ticket with some pocket change and are then told go succeed which is very unlikely. If this were to happen to most of us we would suffer the same failure rates as the statistics currently reveal. I have witnessed the business of mass incarceration, heavily stimulated by harsh sentences imposed during the country's "war on drugs." "We cannot rely on our past accomplishments with only a solution-based focus, we must vote for the change we want.

 Children are expected to survive with incarcerated parents. To lessen the pain and rationalize this cycle, our black boys have accepted incarceration, as a rite of passage into manhood. Today we have more blacks denied the right to vote, because of their criminal records, than the number of blacks denied in 1870.

The late novelist, Ralph Ellison stated, "Our complicated racial past, is a part of our living present. It is a past that speaks even when no one will listen." We must confront the many challenges before us. We have a God-given right to reach our desired potential and sit around humanity's table of choices. We are supposed to have black and minority presidents, mayors, teachers, doctors, scientists, five star generals and entrepreneurs. That is a part of realizing, Dr. Martin Luther King's dream. The Revered Al Sharpton said it best, "We are in the best of times, because we have a black president, in Barrack Obama, a black attorney general, in Eric Holder, and many CEO's -- but in the worst of times, because millions of African-Americans are being locked up and left out, like never before."

It is important to note that, it took many years to create these problems and we must be careful not to create an illusion that they can be corrected overnight. Start with your vote. Vote for your own sake. Vote for the sake of your family and friends. Vote for the sake of your community, state and country.

Be diligent and committed to working together for the common good of all humanity. It will not be easy, but as Romans 8:31 states: If God is for us – who can be against? This country needs us. The one way to combat the darkness is to be the light.

God bless you.
Glen E. Smith Jr.
President/CEO
Elect Protection Group

PREFACE

In 1963, at seven years of age, my Aunt Lilly asked for my mother's permission to take me to the historic March on Washington.

My mother refused. She couldn't handle the idea of something going wrong that would cause her to lose her son.

When I was 11 years old, Dr. Martin Luther King was assassinated. The news released a sullenness into my home ... and neighborhood. I remember going outside the night of Dr. King's murder and standing on the sidewalk with countless people who were also outside of their homes, looking up into the dark sky, staring at the bright, full moon, claiming that it shone the face of Dr. King.

The pain I felt in my soul, at 11 years of age, has never left me and constant reminders of the various forms of assault on my people, has kept a fire burning in the pit of my stomach that I cannot put out.

At 11 years old, I became very clear of what it meant to be the descendant of black slaves in America.

Because I was "bussed-out" to a predominantly white school, I was met by protesters against desegregation and escorted by police officers. On many occasions, my mother would board the city bus and then race to my school, to ensure that I had arrived safely. I often wondered about who protected her as she travelled alone into those conditions.

I refuse to write-off these events, as part of a normal childhood experience. I choose to instead, use these experiences as motivation to achieve my desires, which has included, the publication of this book: to remind all minority communities, relinquished of the past and now living complacently, to wake up! The violation of our civil rights continues. Recent events have retracted our landmark accomplishments from our civil rights movement. This has much to do with our lack of participation in our country's voting process.

Some people believe that since African descendants no longer work on plantations, slavery is completely over in the United States. However, the policies in place enslave Immigrants, driving them to desperate measures to protect their families while using their labor and resources but denying them a path to become a citizen.

I challenge our communities to continue the efforts of the civil rights movement. Fewer and fewer of our people have an informed understanding of the obstacles that were overcome to get to where we are today. I hope to briefly outline the specific historical and current events that demonstrate the importance of involvement in our country's political direction and why efforts must continue for some and start for others.

I would like us to be aware of those affected by the invalidation of Section 4 of the Voting Rights Act of 1965 and to highlight my deep concern for this achievement being summed up as the perpetuation of "racial entitlement."

I would like to educate voters about the importance of midterm elections v. presidential elections and uncover why participation in both is crucial. I would like people to know that 7 billion dollars was invested into the 2012 presidential campaigns in marketing efforts to either sway voters to side with candidates with the best branding, or to discourage voters from participating altogether.

There were 121 million people who voted in the 2012 presidential election and each voter was valued at approximately $55 thousand dollars. Not only is your vote powerful, investors with special interests are willing to pay top dollars to get you to vote for their interests. What will you do with the power of your vote?

I hope to inspire people to honor the sacrifice of our ancestors and all the martyrs who died for our right to vote.

TABLE OF CONTENTS

INTRODUCTION

The first objective of this guide is to provide readers with knowledge of present and historical events, related to the deeply rooted importance of casting one's vote. The second objective is to demystify the election process in the United States of America and enable understanding of our current political climate. The third objective is to share details of current efforts to keep minorities from the polls. Current voting options and information to empower those seeking to restore their voting rights, is also provided.

Chapter 1

OPPRESSION TO EXPRESSION: THE CYCLE

On June 25, 2013, the United States Supreme Court, struck down the heart of the Voting Rights Act of 1965 by a 5-to-4 vote. The preclearance requirement in Section 4 of the Voting Rights Act, mandated that states with a history of discrimination ploys to keep minorities from the polls, "preclear" any changes to voting laws with the United States

Department of Justice, to determine whether minorities are worse off under the proposed change.

The law had applied to nine states - Alabama, Alaska, Arizona, Georgia, Louisiana, Mississippi, South Carolina, Texas and Virginia and to scores of counties and municipalities in other states, including Brooklyn, Manhattan and the Bronx. The decision did not strike down Section 5, but without Section 4, the later section is invalidated, unless the U.S. Congress decides on a new bill that outlines which states will be covered.

The majority vote of the U.S. Supreme Court, found the preclearance formula, unconstitutional, due to a lack of current data to suggest that it was still necessary; the majority took the stance that after 45 years of the Voting Rights Act, there was no longer a need for the protections of preclearance... 45 years had been long enough.

This justification for the majority decision is invalid, as available data indicates that the preclearance formula has successfully blocked discriminatory tactics. For example, between 1982 and 2006, the U.S. Justice Department blocked more than 700 voting change requests that proved to be discriminatory towards voters. In 1965, in the state of Mississippi, white voter registration was nearly 70 percent compared to black voter registration, which stood at 6.7 percent. After preclearance mandates, the percentage of registered black voters increased to 76 percent in 2004, surpassing the white voter registration by four percentage points. This trend had also occurred in other states covered by the preclearance requirement.

The fact that the system has been successful, means that it needs to remain intact. Justice Ginsburg, who was among the dissenting justices, described the decision as undoing the remedy for "first-generation barriers [that enabled] to ballot access" [and has now brought back] "second-generation barriers," which have occurred in the form of racial gerrymandering and laws that enforce at-large voting, in locations with a large black population.

This decision, like the Jim Crow tactics of the past, is likely to keep minority voters from influencing the outcome of the elections. If the U.S. Supreme Court was concerned with addressing the conditions that needed to be met in order for a jurisdiction to require preclearance, it would have addressed Section 4 from a holistic perspective, before leaving a specific demographic of people, vulnerable to the injustices that Section 4 was put in place to block.

The U.S. Congress is the branch of the federal government that is supposed to create laws and decide how to update or change them; the U.S Congress creates laws that reflect the views of the voters who elected them. However, the precedent to invalidate Section 4 was set by the decision of the U.S. Supreme Court, whose jobs is to interpret the laws that the U.S. Congress creates, updates or changes.

Reasonable grounds to believe that the U.S. Congress would have voted to extend Section 4, occurred in 2006, when it was reauthorized by a large majority; the vote outcome was 390 to 33 in the House and unanimous in the Senate.

So, What's the Verdict?

Your vote is powerful and the majority decision made by the conservative justices of the U.S. Supreme Court, displayed this when they chose to strike down Section 4 of the Voting Rights Act. Politicians spend millions of dollars in hopes of securing your vote. People have lost their lives in hopes that their efforts in the civil rights movement, would secure your vote. Laws like Section 4, were put in place to protect your voting rights, because your vote holds value.

If you consider the historical events and rulings that led up to the Voting Rights Act, the decision to strike down Section 4, is an act that mirrors some of our darkest times in American history.

Justice Scalia: Defines "Racial Entitlement"

Justice Scalia explained that the U.S. Supreme Court chose to strike down Section 4 of the Voting Rights Act, because it gave minority's favorable treatment. Although history and available data justifies why Section 4 was created by the U.S Congress, who sought to remedy years of violence and block discriminating measures used to keep minorities from the polls, Justice Scalia described the protection as a "racial entitlement," that the U.S. Congress, would not have the courage to vote against in 2014. Justice Scalia, summarized the achievement of the Voting Rights Act, by stating:

"And this last enactment, not a single vote in the Senate against it. And the House is pretty much the same.... I think it is attributable, very likely attributable, to a phenomenon that is called perpetuation of racial entitlement. It's been written about [Where? It is not in the U.S. Constitution]. Whenever a society adopts racial entitlements, it is very difficult to get out of them through the normal political processes... I don't think there is anything to be gained by any Senator to vote against continuation of this act. And I am fairly confident it will be reenacted in perpetuity unless — unless a court can say it does not comport with the U.S. Constitution... This is not the kind of a question you can leave to Congress.... Even the name of it is wonderful: The Voting Rights Act. Who is going to vote against that in the future?"

Justice Scalia's sentiments are inconsistent with the legal intent behind Section 4, enacted to remedy the specific problem of discrimination against racial minorities that experienced a "perpetuation" of racial insensitivities by the federal and state governments since post Reconstruction-era.

Look in the Mirror: Voting in Post Reconstruction-era

If history is an indicator of whether we are progressing or regressing, then the decision of Justice Scalia and the four other Supreme Court justices that struck down Section 4, cannot be ignored. Their decision is reminiscent of our country's struggles with equality and civil rights.

In 1877, the financial efforts of the federal government through Reconstruction were to put to a halt. The federal troops were pulled out of the South, and state governments, regained full reign over the treatment of minorities in all aspects of their livelihoods, which led to serious ramifications for years to follow prior to passage of the Voting Rights Act. In comparison, the authorization provided in Section 4, to enable the presence of federal examiners to directly register voters and observe polling locations, is no longer authorized by law. This empowers states that were required to preclear any changes to their voting laws and procedures, to use the same measures that were employed in the past to manipulate the outcome of their elections with no legally supported physical or procedural oversight by the federal government.

To ensure that the states had complete control over their policies, laws were immediately removed that protected the rights of blacks.

As long as blacks were able to vote, they would have the power to influence the political process and exercise rights over their living conditions in the South. Jim Crow Laws, replaced the old Black Codes and mass lynchings, violent attacks and the institutions to disempower black men and women continued. The end of the Reconstruction period, was met by a U.S. Supreme Court that began to strike down civil rights laws and amendments that had been accomplished.

In the 1876 case of United States v. Cruikshank, the U.S. Supreme Court ruled that the federal government could not intervene in state or local courts, to isolate blacks from the legal protection of the federal government.

In the 1876 case of United States v. Reese, the U.S. Supreme Court ruled that the federal government could not enforce the right of black voters. In a similar circumstance in which a minority's rights were in question, Justice Scalia, cast the sole vote in favor of allowing the Virginia Military Institute to continue denying admission to women. He later expressed in a 2011 interview that since the U.S. Constitution does not prohibit discrimination on the basis of sex, women have been protected in error under the 14th Amendment.

In 1883, the U.S. Supreme Court declared that the Civil Rights Act of 1875 was unconstitutional. This ruling struck down the U.S. Constitutional rights of equality for all Americans and provided the legal support for "separate, but equal," Jim Crow Laws for the next 70 years.

Justice Clarence Thomas: The Teacher

The story of Clarence Thomas provides one valuable lesson for all voters: Understand a person's policies and ideas about what they believe is best for you and your country, before you support them.

Justice Thomas is the second black American to be appointed to the U.S. Supreme Court. He is one of the five justices on the U.S. Supreme Court that struck down Section 4 of the Voting Rights Act. Justice Thomas has truly reaped the benefits of the law that he struck down and ensured his civil rights as a young black man. He was born in the southern state of Georgia, once declared a required "preclearance" state, for the historical injustices inflicted on blacks' citizens.

A Supreme Court justice is nominated to the Supreme Court by the president in office. President George H.W. Bush nominated Justice

Thomas in 1991 to replace the retiring civil rights icon, Justice Thurgood Marshall, nicknamed, Mr Civil Rights.

Bush's presidential legacy includes vetoing a civil rights bill aimed at enforcing equal work opportunities for minorities. He also signed an anti-drug program into law that expanded the "war on drugs" movement that funded the lucrative business of mass incarceration in the United States, fueled by a disproportionate, majority inmate population of minority males and females.

Bush's decision to appoint Clarence Thomas to the Supreme Court makes sense when looked at from this strategic viewpoint:

Thomas has a record of speaking out against civil rights measures taken by the United States to level the field of opportunity for everyone.

Prior to his nomination, Thomas summed up his thoughts on civil rights activists when he told a reporter that, "all civil rights leaders, "bitch, bitch, bitch, moan and moan, whine and whine."

Even though Thomas acknowledged that he would not have received his Ivy League education and job without affirmative action, he told a reporter that affirmative action places minorities in positions that are above their capabilities. He also publicly revealed that he did not believe that he was qualified for his Supreme Court justice appointment. This is a rare view of Justice Clarence Thomas that I agree with.

So, why would President Bush choose Clarence Thomas? He writes himself off as an affirmative action travesty, who doubts that he is qualified to do his job. He sums up the work of civil rights activists like Rosa Parks, W.E.B. Dubois and Thurgood Marshall as "bitching, moaning and complaining."

If not obvious, Thomas was the prefect choice. President Bush knew that he was not appointing another "Thurgood Marshall," even if it "appeared," that he keeping up with the status quo of a diverse panel.

Justice Thurgood Marshall worked over 60 years to end segregation during his legal profession and won more cases before the Supreme Court than any other American lawyer during his era. He was appointed to the Supreme Court as the first black Supreme Court justice by President Lyndon B. Johnson in 1967. He dedicated his entire legal career to striking down unjust laws and winning social equality for blacks. His most famous case was Brown v. Board of Education of Topeka, Kansas which sparked the end of segregation in the South and the beginning of the civil rights movement. The fight for the equal treatment of blacks opened the door to making the government accountable for the equal treatment of women, war veterans, those with disabilities, plus other races, ethnicities and diverse communities.

To Justice Thurgood Marshall's contrast, Clarence Thomas, has chosen to build a legacy of basing his decisions on cases by judging from an "originalist" view of the U.S. Constitution. This means that his rulings on cases reflect what he believes the original framers of the U.S. Constitution would want. He has used his "originalist" stance to strike down landmark rulings that have helped the United States to progress in granting and protecting the civil rights of all citizens. The problem with Clarence Thomas' "originalist" stance is that the original framers of the U.S. Constitution that spoke of liberty and freedom were only referring to the liberty and freedom of white Christian men: no white Jews, no white Christian women... no one else.

Many of the original framers owned slaves and wrote a U.S. Constitution that supported slavery and declared that blacks were three-fifths of a human being. How could someone of Clarence Thomas' intellect and racial history, knowingly embrace the "originalist" view, that would have never allowed him to sit on the U.S. Supreme Court?

Instead of using his role, to ensure that all people are protected from those who seek to "take their country back," to a time in which the original framers instituted white male supremacy as the law of the land, Thomas, is the poster child for the improper implementation of affirmative action, masquerading as the result of a policy brushed off in recent times as too ambiguous to justify, or just plain wrong in cases where the beneficiaries make a sham of the affirmative obligation of the federal and state governments to repair the wrongs it had committed against a distinct class of people, and the resulting harm to their descendants.

"You do not wipe away the scars of centuries by saying, now, you are free to go where you want, do as you desire, and choose the leaders you please. You do not take a man who for years has been hobbled by chains, liberate him, bring him to the starting line of a race, saying, you are free to compete with all the others, and still justly believe you have been completely fair… whenever this issue of compensatory or preferential treatment for the Negro is raised, some of our friends recoil in horror. The Negro should be granted equality, they agree; but, he should ask for nothing more. On the surface, this appears reasonable, but it is not realistic. For it is obvious that if a man is entering the starting line in a race 300 years after another man, the first would have to perform some impossible feat in order to catch up with his fellow runner."

-President Lyndon B. Johnson

Clarence Thomas is not the first masquerader used by the federal government to halt the progression of civil rights laws. During the American Feminist Movement of the 1960s and 1970s, the leading opponent, Phyllis Schlafly, was a woman who publicly threatened that if an Equal Rights Amendment was passed on behalf of equal opportunity rights for women, it would destroy the role of women in American society. Just like Clarence Thomas, Schlafly was an exception in her time; she was an Ivy League educated, ambitious leader in politics and an outstanding communicator. Despite her benefits from equal opportunity mandates, Schlafly used her power to spread propaganda that manipulated the general public's understanding of the Equal Rights Amendment.

In her publication, The Phyllis Schlafly Report, she used a number of examples detailing how the Equal Rights Amendment, would backfire on women and the nuclear family. For example, Schlafly claimed that the federal government would use affirmative action to ensure that an equal number of women and men were drafted into the U.S. armed services; stirring up fear that 18 year old girls would be forced to fight against their will. Excitement for the opportunities for women turned into fear that equality meant losing basic privileges on the basis for being considered equal to a man.

Schlafly worked to close the doors of opportunities that she walked through. She was powerful and her push for social conservatism led to the defeat of the Equal Rights Amendment. In a Time Magazine interview, she agreed that her greatest achievement in the political field was single-handedly defeating the Equal Rights Amendment. She has a legacy that includes arguing that women need to be paid less so that they can find eligible men to marry. She has also expressed that marriage is synonymous with consensual sex in her argument against women who claim marital rape.

Schlafly's personal and political gains for cultivating the nation's fears about the havoc women would cause with an amendment that enforced their liberty and equality, are debatable. However, like Clarence Thomas, she has made it clear that it is better to stay in your place; the place that the founding fathers, or "originalists" envisioned when they wrote the U.S. Constitution.

Understand a person's policies and ideas about what they believe is best for you and your country, before you support them.

The Haves vs. The Have-Nots

The invested efforts to suppress voters of specific demographics, is not always about, "Black vs. White," it is also about, "The Haves vs. The Have-Nots."

With a growing minority population and Hispanics being the fastest growing demographic in the United States, David and Charles Koch, of Koch Industries, Inc., have realized that efforts to keep minorities from the polls, may not be enough to dilute the interest of the "Radical-Rich vs. Middle-Class/Poor."

The Koch brothers are known for investing in propaganda, and paying lobbyist and legislators millions of dollars to influence state and federal laws that support their interests. The Koch brothers support the Republican Party policies and have invested millions into efforts such as; restricting women's reproductive rights, public school funding and all government funded social welfare programs.

Specific Events: The Struggle For Our Vote

The Civil rights movement had many key players that enabled us to make it to this point. However, there are specific dates in history that led up to the Voting Rights Act:

The right for all minorities groups and women to be included in the liberties, protection and privileges of American citizenship, began with the struggle that African descendants endured for three and a half centuries as slaves. Slavery fueled the economy of the confederate states in the South and provided a wealthy and comfortable way of life for powerful slave owners and Southern legislators who were willing to fight to maintain their way of life, which led to the Civil War of 1861.

President Abraham Lincoln emancipated the slaves in the Confederate states in 1863, as a war tactic, to break the manpower of the southern armies and to demolish their money-making empire. It was not until 1865 when the Civil War was over and won by the Union States in the North, that the government began the Reconstruction program to rebuild the former Confederacy and help freed slaves to acclimate to the changes caused by the war.

The U.S. Congress passed the first Civil Rights Act in 1866 which declared that all people born in the United States were now citizens, without regard to race, color, or previous condition, excluding Indians not taxed. The activities of organizations such as the Ku Klux Klan disobeyed this law by violating the civil rights of blacks for years to follow.

Three U.S. Constitutional Amendments during the Reconstruction period were declared to specifically address the struggling state of blacks in the South:

- The 13th Amendment of 1865 - Outlawed slavery nationwide
- The 14th Amendment of 1868 - Full citizenship rights given to blacks
- The 15th Amendment of 1870 - Protection of Voting Rights for blacks

During Reconstruction, Civil Rights Acts were also added into the U.S. Constitution in 1870, 1871, and 1875. Southern state and local governments instituted Black Codes, which were laws that blocked, or made loopholes to get out of the civil rights laws. In 2014, these tactics have continued to be pursued by state legislators, but had been blocked up until the U.S. Supreme Court struck down Section 4 of the 1965 Voting Rights Act in 2013.

The Voting Rights Act was passed into law during the height of the civil rights movement to prohibit injustices such as, literacy tests and similar "tests or devices" as a prerequisite to voter registration, and to require jurisdictions with significant language minority populations to provide non-English ballots and oral voting instructions.

Black Codes set boundaries on the labor and activities of Blacks with the sole focus of instituting caps on the growth and wealth potential of blacks who faced backlash for asserting their desire to gain economic success (Hmmm... where else do we see this trend in our society?) The Black codes enforced a system similar to the one that existed during slavery. Blacks faced large annual taxes for pursuing occupations other than a farmer or servant, which forced former slaves to return to their slave roles at meager wages.

All Southern states enforced strict employment contract laws and punished white businesses that offered wages higher than caps set for black laborers. Blacks who did not comply were arrested, beat and forced into unpaid labor. Comparatively, in 2014, the resistance to linking minimum wage, to the cost of living, suppresses the wages of the poorest in our society and keeps them dependent on social welfare.

Minors were subject to Apprenticeship Laws that forced them to work on plantations for free. Blacks resisted and argued against the Black Codes. Many Northerners pressured the federal government to respond.

Freedom Summer of 1964 - civil rights workers James Chaney, Andrew Goodman and Michael Schwerner were murdered in Mississippi as they sought out to register black voters.

Bloody Sunday in 1965 - Led by current Georgia congressman, John R. Lewis and members of the Student Nonviolent Coordinating Committee and Southern Christian Leadership Conference, led a voting registration campaign in Alabama that was halted by police officers that shot teargas, and unleashed beatings on the nonviolent protesters and led to the hospitalization of over 50 people. "Bloody Sunday" led to the passage of the Voting Rights Act of 1965 after the group returned to Alabama, determined to peacefully protest the denial of their voting rights.

In 2014, there is currently no federal oversight to ensure that unfair changes to voter ID laws, district lines and other adjustments are taking place that could threaten the rights of minority voters. States have to be caught in the act by the U.S. Justice Department, or challenged by a citizen.

"The [Voting Rights Act] act for nearly 50 years, has helped secure the right to vote for millions of Americans. Today's decision invalidates one of its core provisions- upsets decades of well-established practices that help make sure voting is fair- especially in places where voting discrimination has been historically prevalent."

-President Barack Obama

Chapter 2

GENERAL "MIDTERM" ELECTION

v.

NATIONAL "PRESIDENTIAL" ELECTION

The general "midterm" elections is the time in which voters select the political party that will have the strongest presence in Congress. The

U.S. Congress is the legislative branch of the United States Government and contains the House of Representatives and the Senate. This is important because the U.S. Congress is responsible for creating the laws of the country. If the majority of Congress represents a political party that is different from the president, it will make it very difficult for the president to pass policies that the people elected for.

When the nation votes for electorates that they (knowingly or unknowingly) entrust to vote for their president to achieve a specific agenda, most voters fail to follow up by providing the president with a team of elected representatives in Congress who have similar goals as the president. This causes a divided government, which in most case fails to allow that elected President to take care of what the people expressed they wanted achieved. The current outcome of President Obama's service in office, is the perfect example of a divided government.

After being elected in 2008, President Obama sought passage of a Health Care Bill that were multiple presidents could not pass through Congress. Because of the outcome of the midterm election in 2006, that enabled the Democratic party to represent the majority of Congress, President Obama was able to achieve passage of the Affordable Care Act "Obamacare." Since the 2010 midterm elections, when the Democratic Party became the minority in the U.S. Congress, President Obama has been unsuccessful passing a comprehensive immigration reform policy. In response, some people feel that President Obama has let the Hispanic community down by not keeping his promise to achieve immigration reform, however, during the 2010 midterm elections, it was 11 percent decline in the black vote and the 8 percent decline in the Hispanic vote, that created the opportunity for the conservative Republicans (that do not want immigration reform) to become the majority in the U.S. Congress. Therefore, President Obama has not been able to even vote on immigration reform because we failed to show up at the polls and elect a Democratic majority, that would support his goals.

Politicians will never publicly blame the voters, but clearly, we let ourselves down. This example is an indication of the value of midterm elections and an explanation for why your VOTE matters.

President Obama's agenda included remedying national concerns such as the current recession and immigration reform. However, out of the

61.7 percent of voters that elected the president, only 41 percent voted in the 2010 midterm election. That is approximately a 20 percent reduction in the number of voters and that could have helped to elect the supportive team of Democrats in Congress that President Obama needs to achieve his agenda.

U.S. Congress

The midterm elections are held two years into the four year term of the current presidency. The midterm election is when all seats in the House of Representatives and one-third of the members of the Senate are elected. The members of the House of Representatives do their jobs for two years. Senators do their jobs for six years.

Presidents Obama has been dealing with a Republican majority in the U.S. Congress that has rejected almost everything that he set on political agenda.

Who is to Blame?

The blame lies on the 20 percent of voters that did not vote in the 2010 midterm election to ensure that their president had a team of legislators behind him that would enable him to pass his policies. It is that simple.

We must learn from this mistake and correct the error of the 2010 midterm election, by marching to the poles like never before.

FYI:

Many state and local positions are voted on during the midterm election as well. Elected individuals will represent the opinions of the majority vote on policies such as public education, healthcare, taxes, wages, social welfare and corporate welfare programs. Only citizens that participate in the voting process will affect the outcome of decisions made at the local, state, and federal levels.

The source for a comprehensive list of the offices that are up for election and directions for how to cast your vote are available through your local county, parish or district elections office and website.

States vary in the terminology for this division of government. For example, The Florida

Division for Elections website, directs voters to their Supervisor of Elections website by county of residence. Therefore, a resident of Orange County Florida, is directed to the Supervisor of Elections Orange County Florida website.

However, in Louisiana, voting information is found by going to the Louisiana Secretary of State website and then clicking on a link that connects to the Louisiana Elections Division website for voter registration information.

DON'T BE DISCOURAGED by the differences in the voting directions that are provided according to your United States residence. Take the time to learn and understand the steps that are appropriate for your situation.

There are not-for-profit support groups that provide a direct link to the voting process for citizens that need assistance. For example, The League of Women Voters is an organization that works to provide a clear understanding of the voting process, plus opportunities to get involved in their fight to improve the U.S. government and engage all citizens in the decisions that have an impact on the nation.

The League of Women Voters operates at the national, state and local levels in all 50 states, including the District of Columbia, The Virgin Islands and Hong Kong. Created from the movement that secured the right to vote for women, their values are based on their history of advocating participation in the democracy for American citizens regardless of political party affiliation.

Chapter 3

READY TO VOTE?
TAKE ACTION!

Our To-Do List:

2014 - We must march to the poles. The outcome will determine what President Obama and the president of 2016 will be able to accomplish.

2016 - We will vote for the new president. This president will have the authority to appoint members to the Supreme Court and may change the recent injustices performed by rulings of the Supreme Court

2018 - We will vote in the midterm election to determine the majority opinion in Congress and ultimately what the current president is able to do.

2020 - We will vote for the new president. This president will have the authority to appoint members to the Supreme Court, which history has shown will either negatively or positively affect us.

Our participation in the voting process will determine the political, economic and social climate in the United States for the next six years.

To vote in U.S. elections you must be:

- A citizen of the United States on the date of the election in which you wish to vote
- Minimum 18 years of age on Election Day (17 years of age is permitted in some states for the primary election if the 18th birthdate is on or before the general election)

You must be a registered voter to vote in the midterm or presidential elections. You can register or download a form online, or you can request a postage paid form. Your initial registration information will last a lifetime. If you need to change your name, address, or party enrollment, submit a new registration application.

What is an Absentee Ballot?

Absentee voting involves voting on a ballot received by mail or picked up by or for a person who is unable to go to the polls to vote during early voting or Election Day. A request must be made to receive an absentee ballot. A request covers all elections through the end of the calendar year for the second ensuing regularly scheduled general election.

The absentee voting process applies to you if you are:

- An active duty member of the U.S. Armed Services, Merchant Marine or Activated National Guard or a family member (spouse or dependent)
- A U.S. citizen residing outside of the U.S.
- You will be absent from your city or town on election day

- You have a physical disability that prevents your voting at the polling location
- Due to religious beliefs
- Some states provide absentee ballots regardless of the reason for request

Seek out your local county, parish or district elections office address or website to learn about the options available to you.

What Is the "Primary" Stage of the "Midterm" Election?

Primary elections are held to determine which candidates will be on the midterm election ballots. Voters choose from candidates competing for various positions in the primary round of elections.

The winners from the midterm round of elections take their respective positions at the local, state and federal levels of government.

The deadline to vote in the primary elections varies by state. For a comprehensive list of the offices that are up for election, voting dates, or for directions on how to cast your vote, seek out your local county, parish, or district elections office address or website.

Same Day Registration *(SDR)*

In most states, many qualified voters are turned away from the polls on Election Day because they did not register to vote before the registration deadline.

In states that offer same-day registration, (also called "Election Day" registration) unregistered, qualified voters can register to vote at their polling place or election clerk's office on Election Day. To register, potential voters must supply proof of residency verifying that they are able to vote in that state, and a form of personal identification.

Currently, ten states – Colorado, Connecticut, Idaho, Iowa, Maine, Minnesota, Montana, New Hampshire, Wisconsin, and Wyoming – and the District of Columbia offer some form of SDR.

What Political Party Should I Vote For?

America's two major political parties are the Republican and Democratic parties.

It is important to understand the vision and policies that divide the political groups. Take the time to read, listen, or watch videos about the various political parties and their representatives before casting your vote.

The Republican and Democrat parties have VERY different views:

Issue	Views
Abortion:	Democrats Support Republican Oppose
LBGT marriage:	Democrats Support Republican Oppose
Tax cuts:	Democrats Oppose Republicans Support
Voluntary prayer in school:	Democrats Oppose Republicans Support

Gun control: Democrats Support
Republicans Oppose

Minimum wage hike: Democrats Support
Republicans Oppose

Affirmative action: Democrats Support
Republicans Oppose

Chapter 4

I'm a Convicted Felon. How Do I Restore My Right to Vote?

A Refocused Movement For Racial Justice In America

The Brennan Center for Justice at the New York University Law School reports that 4.4 citizens work, and raise families in the United States and are unable vote because of a past criminal conviction. Across the country, 13 percent of black men have lost their right to vote, which is seven times the national average and the reason that many people support felony disenfranchisement reform.

The restoration of voting rights, may strengthen social ties to the community and positively affect minorities often caught in the cycle of poverty and drugs, which in often leads to incarceration.

When a state bans a citizen from voting, the steps to regain the right to vote are governed by state law. Therefore, the best source of reliable information is the appropriate state office.

In many states, felony disenfranchisement laws are still on the books and the current scope of these policies are not only too significant to ignore, it is also too unjust to tolerate. Although well over a century has passed since post Reconstruction states used these measures to strip African Americans of their most fundamental rights; the impact of felony disenfranchisement on modern communities of color remains both disproportionate and unacceptable. Throughout America, 2.2 million black citizens, or nearly one in 13 African-American adults, are banned from voting because of these laws. In three states– Florida, Kentucky, and Virginia– that ratio climbs to one in five."

-U.S. Attorney General Eric Holder, J.D.

Listed below are the websites for the states and territories that have posted information on the process for restoring the right to vote as of August 2014. Contact the state for the most current information:

Alabama:

http://www.pardons.state.al.us/ALABPP/Main/ALABpp%20MAIN.htm

Alaska:

http://www.elections.alaska.gov/vi_restore_info.php
http://www.correct.state.ak.us/rehabilitation-reentry
http://www.correct.state.ak.us/pnp/pdf/808.08.pdf

American Samoa:

http://www.americansamoaelectionoffice.org/

Arizona:

http://www.azsos.gov/election/VoterRegistration.htm
http://www.clerkofcourt.maricopa.gov/faxondemand/300.pdf

Arkansas:

http://www.sos.arkansas.gov/elections/Pages/voterResources.aspx
http://www.arbop.org/

California:

http://www.sos.ca.gov/elections/sharing-ideas/a-voting-guide-for-inmates.pdf
http://www.sos.ca.gov/elections/sharing-ideas/voting-rights-californians.htm

Colorado:

http://www.sos.state.co.us/pubs/elections/FAQs/VotingAndConviction.html

Connecticut:

http://www.sots.ct.gov/sots/cwp/view.asp?a=3179&Q=533854&sotsNav=|
http://www.ct.gov/doc/lib/doc/PDF/VotingRightsEnglish.pdf

Delaware:

http://elections.delaware.gov/services/voter/felons.shtml

District of Columbia:

http://www.dcboee.org/faq/voter_reg.asp

Florida:

https://fpc.state.fl.us/clemencyOverview.shtml

Georgia:

http://www.dcor.state.ga.us/pdf/ReentrySkillsBuildingHandbook-English.pdf

http://sos.ga.gov/index.php/elections/faq

Guam:

http://gec.guam.gov/2011/11/16/for-voters/

Hawaii:

http://hawaii.gov/elections/factsheets/html/fsvs509.htm/download

Idaho:

http://www.idahovotes.gov/VoterReg/REG_FAQ.HTM

Illinois:

http://www.elections.il.gov/DocDisplay.aspx?Doc=Downloads/ElectionInformation/PDF/registervote.pdf&Title=Registering to Vote in Illinois

http://www.elections.il.gov/DocDisplay.aspx?Doc=Downloads/VotingInformation/PDF/R-19.pdf&Title=Illinois

Indiana:

http://www.in.gov/sos/elections/2403.htm

Iowa:

https://governor.iowa.gov/constituent-services/restoration-of-citizenship-rights/

Kentucky:

http://justice.ky.gov/default.htm

Louisiana:

http://www.sos.louisiana.gov/tabid/68/Default.aspx

Maine:

http://www.maine.gov/sos/cec/elec/resident.htm

Maryland:

http://www.elections.state.md.us/voter_registration/restoration.html

Massachusetts:

http://www.sec.state.ma.us/ele/eleifv/howreg.htm

Michigan:

http://www.michigan.gov/sos/0,1607,7-127-29836-202492--F,00.html

Minnesota:

http://www.sos.state.mn.us/index.aspx?page=1610
http://www.sos.state.mn.us/index.aspx?page=204

Mississippi:

http://www.sos.ms.gov/elections_voter_info_center.aspx

Missouri:

http://www.sos.mo.gov/elections/goVoteMissouri/questions.aspx#3_2

Montana:

http://sos.mt.gov/Elections/Vote/index.asp#who

Nebraska:

http://www.sos.state.ne.us/elec/voter_info.html

Nevada:

http://nvsos.gov/index.aspx?page=86

New Hampshire:

http://sos.nh.gov/Felons.aspx

New Jersey:

http://www.state.nj.us/state/elections/voting-information.html#2

New Mexico:

http://www.sos.state.nm.us/Voter_Information/

New York:

http://www.elections.ny.gov/VotingRegister.html

North Carolina:
http://www.ncsbe.gov/ncsbe/registering-to-vote

North Dakota:
http://www.nd.gov/sos/electvote/voting/voter-qualifi.html

Northern Mariana Islands:
http://www.votecnmi.gov.mp/index.php/component/content/article/53-voter/173-voters-pamphlet

Ohio:
http://www.sos.state.oh.us/sos/elections/Voters/FAQ/voterEligibility.aspx

Oklahoma:
http://www.ok.gov/elections/Voter_Registration/Voter_Registration_Application_Form/

Oregon:
http://sos.oregon.gov/voting/Pages/voteinor.aspx

Pennsylvania:

http://www.votespa.com/portal/server.pt?open=514&obj ID=1174123&mode=2

Puerto Rico:

http://www.ceepur.org/

Rhode Island:

https://sos.ri.gov/elections/voters/register/

South Carolina:

http://www.scvotes.org/
south_carolina_voter_registration_information

South Dakota:

https://sdsos.gov/elections-voting/voting/register-to-vote/default.aspx

Tennessee:

http://state.tn.us/sos/election/restoration.htm

Texas:

http://www.sos.state.tx.us/elections/voter/reqvr.shtml

Utah:

http://vote.utah.gov/vote/

https://secure.utah.gov/voterreg/index.html

Vermont:

https://www.sec.state.vt.us/elections/frequently-asked-questions/voter-registration.aspx#faq-4356

Virginia:

https://commonwealth.virginia.gov/applications/clemency

Virgin Islands:

http://www.vivote.gov/content/register-vote

Washington:

https://wei.sos.wa.gov/agency/osos/en/voters/Pages/felons_and_voting_rights.aspx

West Virginia:

http://www.sos.wv.gov/elections/voterinformation/Frequently AskedQuestions/Pages/Voter_Registration_FAQ.aspx

Wisconsin:

http://gab.wi.gov/node/2473

Wyoming:

http://bop.state.wy.us/votingrights/votingrights.htm

Chapter 5

KEEP IT MOVING: THE CIVIL RIGHTS MOMENTUM

Your quality of life and the people that you love, are affected by at least some of the topics listed below. Take the time to learn about how these and other issues that concern you, are being discussed or regulated by your local, state and federal legislators.

Collectively, our votes determine the outcome of the laws that have an impact on our everyday lives. Your vote is powerful.

- Civil Rights
- Voting Rights
- Poverty
- Education
- Job availability and minimum wage
- Healthcare
- Social Welfare and Corporate Welfare
- Mass Incarceration of Minorities - In 2014, Blacks are 13 percent of the U.S. population and 70 percent of the prison population
- LGBT Rights
- Disability Rights
- Veteran Rights
- Racial Profiling and Violent Attacks/Murders

- Cycle/Trap of Poverty: poverty, drugs, jail
- Affirmative Action

"A people without the knowledge of their past history, origin, and culture, is like a tree without roots."

-Civil Rights Activist, Marcus Garvey

For Inquiries Contact:

Voices Impacting America Inc
A Not-For-Profit, Civil Rights Organization
Founded by J.W. Cherry III
jwc@voicesimpactingamerica.org
(888) 500-4227

Marketing Department
marketing@voicesimpactingamerica.org

Media Department
media@voicesimpactingamerica.org

Speaking Events

speaking@voicesimpactingamerica.org

Book Orders

books@voicesimpactingamerica.org

BIBLIOGRAPHY

African Americans: Many Rivers to Cross. Dir. Henry Louis Gates, Jr., Ph.D. Perf. Henry Louis Gates, Jr. PBS (DIRECT), 2014. DVD.

Altman, Linda J. The American Civil Rights Movement. New Jersey: Enslow Publishers, Inc., 2004. Print.

"American Civil Liberties Union." Promoting Access | American Civil Liberties Union. Comp. American Civil Liberties Union. American Civil Liberties Union, n.d. Web. 11 Aug. 2014. <https://www.aclu.org/voting-rights/promoting-access>.

Barnes, Robert. "Supreme Court Stops Use of Key Part of Voting Rights Act." Supreme Court Stops Use of Key Part of Voting Rights Act - The Washington Post. The Washington Post, 25 June 2013. Web. 11 Aug. 2014. <http://www.washingtonpost.com/politics/supreme-court-stops-use-of-key-part-of-voting-rights-act/2013/06/25/26888528-dda5-11e2-b197-f248b21f94c4_story.html>.

Blake, Aaron. "Clarence Thomas Compares Affirmative Action Policies to Segregation." Clarence Thomas Compares Affirmative Action Policies to Segregation - The Washington Post. The Washington Post, 24 June 2013. Web. 11 Aug. 2014. <http://www.washingtonpost.com/blogs/post-politics/wp/2013/06/24/clarence-thomas-compares-affirmative-action-policies-to-segregation/>.

Blake, John. "Three Questions for Clarence Thomas." Three Questions for Clarence Thomas - CNN.com. CNN, 9 June 2013. Web. 24 July 2014. <http://www.cnn.com/2013/06/09/us/clarence-thomas-three-questions/>.

Blow, Charles M. "Vulnerability of the Vote." Vulnerability of the Vote - NYTimes.com. The New York Times Company, 27 Feb. 2013. Web. 11 Aug. 2014. <http://www.nytimes.com/2013/02/28/opinion/blow-vulnerability-of-the-vote.html?_r=0>.

Bravin, Jess. "Court Upends Voting Rights Act." Supreme Court Upends Voting Rights Act - WSJ. Wall

Street Journal, 25 June 2013. Web. 11 Aug. 2014.
<http://online.wsj.com/news/articles/SB1000142412788
732346980457852136384096203 2>.

The College of Architecture, Planning and Design. "Civil
Rights Acts of 1866, 1870, 1871, 1875." Civil Rights Acts
of 1866, 1870, 1871, 1875. The College of Architecture,
Planning and Design, n.d. Web. 19 Aug. 2014.
<http://www.arch.ksu.edu/jwkplan/law/civil%20rights%
20acts%20of%201866,%201870,%201871,%201875.htm>
.

Cornell University Law School. "Affirmative Action."
Affirmative Action | Wex Legal Dictionary /
Encyclopedia | LII / Legal Information Institute. Cornell
University Law School Legal Information Institute, n.d.
Web. 11 Aug. 2014.
<http://www.law.cornell.edu/wex/affirmative_action>.

Dale, Charles V. "Federal Affirmative Action Law: A
Brief History." CRS Report for Congress. Foreign Press
Centers: U.S. Department of State Bureau of Public
Affairs, 13 Sept. 2005. Web. 20 Aug. 2014.
<http://fpc.state.gov/documents/organization/53577.pdf>.

Davidson, Amy. "The New Yorker." In Voting Rights, Scalia Sees a "Racial Entitlement" - The New Yorker. The New Yorker, 28 Feb. 2013. Web. 11 Aug. 2014. <http://www.newyorker.com/news/amy-davidson/in-voting-rights-scalia-sees-a-racial-entitlement>.

"Elections." Congress for Kids: [Elections]: The Inauguration. Comp. The Dirksen Congressional Center. The Dirksen Congressional Center, n.d. Web. 11 Aug. 2014. <http://www.congressforkids.net/Elections_inauguration.htm>.

"Feature Causes Of The Civil War." Causes Of The Civil War | History Detectives | PBS. Comp. PBS Station. PBS Station, n.d. Web. 1 Aug. 2014. <http://www.pbs.org/opb/historydetectives/feature/causes-of-the-civil-war/>.

"Felon Voting Pros and Cons." State Felon Voting Laws - Felon Voting - ProCon.org. Comp. Pros and Cons of Controversial Issues. ProCon.org, 15 July 2014. Web. 24 July 2014. <http://felonvoting.procon.org/view.resource.php?resourceID=000286>.

Gamboa, Suzanne. "50 Years after Martin Luther King, Marchers Gather in Capital." 50 Years after Martin Luther King, Marchers Gather in Capital | TheGrio. Associated Press, 22 Aug. 2013. Web. 11 Aug. 2014. <http://thegrio.com/2013/08/22/50-years-after-martin-luther-king-marchers-gather-in-capital/>.

Gamboa, Suzanne. "Marching for King's Dream: 'The Task Is Not Done'." Marching for King's Dream: 'The Task Is Not Done' | TheGrio. Associated Press, 24 Aug. 2013. Web. 11 Aug. 2014. <http://thegrio.com/2013/08/24/marching-for-kings-dream-the-task-is-not-done/>.

History.com. "Black Codes." Black Codes - Black History - HISTORY.com. A+E Networks Corp, n.d. Web. 11 Aug. 2014. <http://www.history.com/topics/black-history/black-codes>.

Krever, Mick. "Two Years after Trayvon Martin Killing, Human Rights Lawyer Says America 'burdened with a Legacy of Slavery'." Two Years after Trayvon Martin Killing, Human Rights Lawyer Says America 'burdened with a Legacy of Slavery' – Amanpour - CNN.com Blogs.

CNN, 26 Feb. 2014. Web. 11 Aug. 2014. <http://amanpour.blogs.cnn.com/2014/02/26/two-years-after-trayvon-martin-killing-human-rights-lawyer-says-america-burdened-with-a-legacy-of-slavery/?iref=allsearch>.

Kristof, Nicholas. "Is a Hard Life Inherited?." Is a Hard Life Inherited? - NYTimes.com. The New York Times Company, 9 Aug. 2014. Web. 9 Aug. 2014. <http://www.nytimes.com/2014/08/10/opinion/sunday/nicholas-kristof-is-a-hard-life-inherited.html?src=recg&module=Ribbon&version=origin&region=Header&action=click&contentCollection=Recommended&pgtype=article>.

Mandery, Evan J. "End College Legacy Preferences." End College Legacy Preferences - NYTimes.com. The New York Times Company, 24 Apr. 2014. Web. 24 July 2014. <http://www.nytimes.com/2014/04/25/opinion/end-college-legacy-preferences.html?_r=0>.

Nasso, Christine. Voting Rights. Farmington Hills: Gale and Greenhaven Press, 2008. Print.

Neale, Thomas H. "CRS Report for Congress: The Electoral College: How It Works in Contemporary Presidential Elections." Foreign Press Center: U.S. Department of State Bureau of Public Affairs. U.S. Department of State: Government and Finance Division, 8 Sept. 2003. Web. 11 Aug. 2014. <http://fpc.state.gov/documents/organization/28109.pdf>.

"Political Parties." BrainPOP | Social Studies | Learn about Political Parties. Comp. BrainPop. BrainPop, n.d. Web. 24 July 2014. <http://www.brainpop.com/socialstudies/usgovernment andlaw/politicalparties/preview.weml>.

"Regaining the Right to Vote." United States Department of Justice. Comp. United States Department of Justice. United States Department of Justice, n.d. Web. 24 July 2014. http://www.justice.gov/crt/about/vot/restore_vote.php>.

Scardino, Franco. U.S. Government & Politics. New York: Penguin Group, 2008. Print.

Schaffrey, Mary, and Melanie Fonder. American Government. Second ed. New York: Penguin Group, 2005. Print.

Schechter, Patricia A., Ph.D. "The Anti-Lynching Pamphlets of Ida B. Wells, 1892-1920." Ida. B. Wells, 1862-1931. Illinois Historical Digitization Projects: Northern Illinois University Libraries, n.d. Web. 11 Aug. 2014. <http://dig.lib.niu.edu/gildedage/idabwells/pamphlets.html>.

Sharp, Anne W. A Dream Deferred: The Jim Crow Era. Detroit: Thomas Gale, 2005. Print.

Sobel, Syl, J.D., and. How the U.S. Government Works. Second ed. New York: Barron's, 2012. Print.

Stiglitz, Joseph E. The Price of Inequality. New York: W.W. Norton & Company, 2012. Print.

Strauss, Valerie. "Why Race-based Affirmative Action in College Admissions Still Matters." Why Race-based Affirmative Action in College Admissions Still Matters - The Washington Post. The Washington Post, 11 Aug.

2014. Web. 11 Aug. 2014.
<http://www.washingtonpost.com/blogs/answer-sheet/wp/2014/08/11/why-race-based-affirmative-action-in-college-admissions-still-matters/>.

Sullivan, Sean. "Everything You Need to Know about the Supreme Court Voting Rights Act Decision." Everything You Need to Know about the Supreme Court Voting Rights Act Decision - The Washington Post. The Washington Post, 25 June 2013. Web. 11 Aug. 2014. <http://www.washingtonpost.com/blogs/the-fix/wp/2013/02/27/the-supreme-court-voting-rights-act-case-explained/>.

The Civil Rights Movement. Ed. Salem Press. Vol. 2. Pasadena: Salem Press, Inc., 2000. Print.

"Voting Rights Act." Voting Rights Act | Wex Legal Dictionary / Encyclopedia | LII / Legal Information Institute. Comp. Cornell University Law School. Cornell University Law School: Legal Information Institute, n.d. Web. 11 Aug. 2014. <http://www.law.cornell.edu/wex/voting_rights_act>.

Weiser, Wendy R., and Erik Opsal. "Restoring Voting Rights." Brennan Center for Justice. Brennan Center for Justice at New York University School of Law, 17 June 2014. Web. 24 July 2014. <http://www.brennancenter.org/issues/restoring-voting-rights>.